First World War
and Army of Occupation
War Diary
France, Belgium and Germany

51 DIVISION
152 Infantry Brigade,
Brigade Machine Gun Company
16 January 1916 - 28 February 1918

WO95/2868/3

The Naval & Military Press Ltd
www.nmarchive.com
Published in association with The National Archives

Published by

The Naval & Military Press Ltd

Unit 10 Ridgewood Industrial Park,

Uckfield, East Sussex,

TN22 5QE England

Tel: +44 (0) 1825 749494

www.naval-military-press.com

www.nmarchive.com

This diary has been reprinted in facsimile from the original. Any imperfections are inevitably reproduced and the quality may fall short of modern type and cartographic standards.

© **Crown Copyright**
Images reproduced by permission of The National Archives, London, England, 2015.

Contents

Document type	Place/Title	Date From	Date To
Heading	WO95/2868 Brigade Machine Gun Co Jan 1916-Feb 1918		
Heading	51st Division 152nd Infy Bde 152nd Machine Gun Coy. Jan 1916-Feb 1918		
Heading	War Diary Of 152nd Infantry Brigade Machine Gun Company From 16th January 1916 To 31st January 1916		
War Diary	In The Field	16/01/1916	31/01/1916
Heading	War Diary Of 152nd Infantry Brigade Machine Gun Company From 1st February 1916 To 29th February 1916 Vol II		
Heading	War Diary Of 152nd Brigade Machine Gun Coy. From 1st February To 29th February 1916		
War Diary	In The Field	01/02/1916	29/02/1916
Heading	War Diary Of 152nd Infantry Brigade Machine Gun Company From 1st March 1916 To 31st March 1916		
War Diary	In The Field	01/03/1916	30/04/1916
Heading	War Diary Of 152nd Bde MG Coy From 1st To 31st May 1916		
War Diary	In The Field	01/05/1916	31/05/1916
Heading	War Diary Of 152nd Bde. Machine Gun Coy. From 1st To 30th June 1916		
War Diary	In The Field	01/06/1916	30/06/1916
Heading	152nd Brigade Machine Gun Company July 1916		
Heading	War Diary Of 152nd Machine Gun Company July 1916		
War Diary	In The Field	01/07/1916	31/07/1916
Heading	152nd Brigade Machine Gun Company August 1916		
War Diary	In The Field	01/08/1916	31/08/1916
Miscellaneous	Headquarters, 152nd Inf. Brigade.	05/09/1916	05/09/1916
Heading	War Diary Of 152nd Machine Gun Company From 1st September 1916 To 30th September 1916		
War Diary	Field	01/09/1916	30/09/1916
Heading	War Diary Of 152nd Company Machine Gun Corps From 1st October 1916 To 31st October 1916		
War Diary		01/10/1916	17/10/1916
War Diary	Field	18/10/1916	31/10/1916
Heading	War Diary Of 152nd Company Machine Gun Corps November 1916		
War Diary	In The Field	01/11/1916	30/11/1916
Heading	War Diary Of 152nd Company Machine Gun Corps From 1st December 1916 To 31st December 1916		
War Diary	In The Field	01/12/1916	31/12/1916
Heading	War Diary Of 152nd Company Machine Gun Corps From 1st January 1917 To 31st January 1917		
War Diary	In The Field	01/01/1917	31/01/1917
Heading	War Diary Of 152nd Machine Gun Company From 1st February 1917 To 28th February 1917		
War Diary	In The Field	01/02/1917	28/02/1917
Heading	War Diary Of 152nd Machine Gun Company From 1st March 1917 To 31st March 1917		

War Diary	In The Field	01/03/1917	30/03/1917
Heading	War Diary Of 152nd Machine Gun Company For April 1917		
War Diary	In The Field	01/04/1917	30/04/1917
Heading	War Diary Of 152nd Company Machine Gun Corps May 1917.		
War Diary	In The Field	01/05/1917	31/05/1917
Map	Map		
Heading	War Diary Of 152nd Company Machine Gun Corps June 1917		
War Diary		01/06/1917	30/06/1917
War Diary		01/07/1917	31/07/1917
Heading	War Diary Of 152nd Machine Gun Company 1st August 1917 To 31st August 1917		
War Diary	In The Field	31/07/1917	31/08/1917
Miscellaneous			
Map	Pilckem		
Miscellaneous	Pilckem 1/10000		
War Diary	In The Field	01/09/1917	30/09/1917
Miscellaneous	Report On Action Of Barrage Batteries During Secret Operations		
Miscellaneous	Appendix "B" To September War Diary		
Map	Map		
Heading	War Diary For October 1917 Of 152nd Coy M.G.C		
War Diary	In The Field	01/10/1917	31/10/1917
War Diary	152nd Brigade 51st Division 152nd Machine Gun Company November 1917		
War Diary	In The Field	01/11/1917	30/11/1917
Miscellaneous	Headquarters, 152nd Infantry Brigade. Appendix A	28/11/1917	28/11/1917
Miscellaneous	152nd Coy. M.G.C.		
Diagram etc	To Superimpose On Sheet 57c N.E		
Heading	152nd Coy. M.G.C War Diary For December 1917		
War Diary	In The Field	01/12/1917	30/12/1917
Heading	War Diary Of 152nd Co. M.G Corps From 1st To 31st Jan 1918 Vol 25		
War Diary	In The Field	01/01/1918	29/01/1918
Heading	War Diaries 152 Co M.G.C From 1st To 28th Feb 1918		
War Diary	In The Field	01/02/1918	28/02/1918

(3) WO 95/2868

Brigade Machine Gun Co.

Jan 1916 — Feb 1918

51ST DIVISION
152ND INFY BDE.

152ND MACHINE GUN COY.

JAN 1916 - FEB 1918

WAR DIARY.
of
152nd Infantry Brigade Machine Gun Company.

From
16th January 1916.
to
31st January 1916.

Vol I

CONFIDENTIAL
No. 134
152nd INF. BDE.

152nd Bde. in G. Coy. — Army Form C. 2118.

Confidential

WAR DIARY
—OR—
INTELLIGENCE SUMMARY.
(Erase heading not required.)

Instructions regarding War Diaries and Intelligence Summaries are contained in F. S. Regs., Part II. and the Staff Manual respectively. Title Pages will be prepared in manuscript.

Place	Date 1916	Hour	Summary of Events and Information	Remarks and references to Appendices
In the field	16th July		Company formed with Headquarters at Mollien-au-Bois.	
	17th "		Training in rest billets at Mollien-au-Bois.	
	19th "		"	
	20th "		Brigade Transport inspection by G.O.C. 13th Corps.	
	20/4 "		Company training in rest billets at Mollien-au-Bois.	
	26th "			
	27th "		Inspection by G.O.C. 51st (H) Division.	
	28th "		Training in rest billets at Mollien-au-Bois.	
	31st "		"	

Mundayfadn
Captain,
OC
152nd Brigade in G. Coy.

WAR DIARY

of

152nd Infantry Brigade Machine Gun Company.

From
1st February, 1916.
To
29th February 1916.

Vol II

"Confidential"

War Diary.
of
152nd. Brigade Machine Gun Coy.

From 1st. February to 29th. February 1916.

[signature]
Captain.
O.C.
152nd. Brigade M. Gun Coy.

Confidential

152nd Brigade M.Gun. Coy. **WAR DIARY**

Army Form C. 2118

of

INTELLIGENCE SUMMARY

(Erase heading not required.)

Instructions regarding War Diaries and Intelligence Summaries are contained in F.S. Regs., Part II. and the Staff Manual respectively. Title Pages will be prepared in manuscript.

Place	Date 1916	Hour	Summary of Events and Information	Remarks and references to Appendices
In the field	Feb 7th		Company training in rest billets at Méricourt-au-Bois.	
	8th		Move to billets at Corbie.	
	9th to 28th		Company training in rest billets at Corbie.	
	29th		Move to billets at Méricourt-au-Bois.	

M. Wardenfarn.
Captain,
O.C.
152nd Inf. Bde. M.Gun. Coy.

Vol III

CONFIDENTIAL
No. 134
152nd INF. BDE.

WAR DIARY.

of

152nd Infantry Brigade Machine Gun Company.

From
1st March, 1916.
To
31st March, 1916.

Confidential

152nd Inf. Bde. M.G. Coy. **WAR DIARY** Army Form C. 2118

Instructions regarding War Diaries and Intelligence Summaries are contained in F.S. Regs., Part II. and the Staff Manual respectively. Title Pages will be prepared in manuscript.

INTELLIGENCE SUMMARY
(Erase heading not required.)

CONFIDENTIAL No. 134
152nd INF. BDE.

Place	Date 1916	Hour	Summary of Events and Information	Remarks and references to Appendices
In the field	March 1st 2nd 3rd 4th 5th 6th 7th 8th 9th 10th 11th 12th 13th 14th 15th		In rest billets Molliens-au-Bois. Move to Beauval. In rest billets Beauval. Move to Oppy. Move to Maroeuil. Relieved the 43rd French Light Infry. Regiment & Machine Guns. Ten guns in support & six guns in Bde. Reserve at Maroeuil. Headquarters of Company in Maroeuil. Quiet in support line. Nothing to report. Twelve Guns in support & 4 Guns in Bde. Reserve at Maroeuil. Headquarters of Company in trenches. Quiet in support. Nothing to report. Indirect fire scheme. 500 rounds at 17 D 0.2 to 17 D 5.1. 500 rounds at 17 A 9.5 to 17 A 4.1. 1000 rounds at 17 D 7.0 to 18 A 2.5. Between our 51 D. N.W.1. German replied with rifle & machine gun fire.	

Winberg Capt.

"Confidential"
152nd Inf. Bde. H.Q. C.S.
WAR DIARY
or
INTELLIGENCE SUMMARY

Army Form C. 2118

CONFIDENTIAL
No. 134
152nd Inf. Bde.

Place	Date 1916	Hour	Summary of Events and Information	Remarks and references to Appendices
Intelligence	19/20	7.30	Indirect fire scheme. Ranging on junction of trenches at 17D.4.2. 500 rounds fired.	
			" 250 rounds on 27.B.3.7 to 17D.4.2. New works being carried out at this point.	
			" 500 rounds on Bazan 17D.3.7 to 17D.10.2.	
			" 500 " " trail 17D.7.0. to 18A.2.8.	
			" 5.00 " " Bazan 17A.9.5. to 18A.4.1.	
	20/21		Combined Indirect fire scheme with two guns on road 17D.7.0 to 18A.2.8. — 1,750 rounds fired.	
	21/22			
	22/23		Indirect fire scheme. Ranging fire on 17D.7.0. 500 rounds fired.	
	23/24		" 1,500 rounds on trenches 11D.7½ to 12C.4.4.	
	24/25		" on trenches 17.D.4.2. and trenches between 11D.7½.16½.7.C.4.4. 750 rounds at each target. When fire was opened a red light was put up in direction of target.	
			A noise like that of a steam engine was heard at 15.D.1.1. about 11pm coming from direction of enemy, about 2.30am explosion of mine was heard, followed by heavy bombing on our left front.	

J. Munro Tait, Capt.

Confidential
157th Inf. Bde. M.G. Coy.   WAR DIARY or INTELLIGENCE SUMMARY

Army Form C. 2118
CONFIDENTIAL No. 134
152nd INF. BDE.

Place	Date 1916	Hour	Summary of Events and Information	Remarks and references to Appendices
Zillebeke	25/26		Continued Indirect fire scheme with two guns on communication trenches 17.A.9.5. to 18A.4.1. and 17.D.4.2. to 17.D.5.1. - 2,700 rounds fired.	
	26/27		Quiet in support line, nothing to report.	
	27/8		Indirect fire scheme on communication trench 17.D.4.2.	
			" with three guns on 11A.3.2. to 11A.9.9, 17D.7.0 to 18A.2.9. - 11D.7.1 to 12B.6.4., 17D.4.2 to 17D.5.1, 17A.9.5. to 18.A.4.1	
			" with two guns on 23B.3.7 to 17D.4.2. - 3,750 rounds fired.	
			" " " " 24A.1.1 to 17D.4.2, 17D.4.2 to B.1.1250 " "	
	28/29		Quiet in Support, nothing to report.	
	29/30		Indirect fire scheme. Ranging with guns on 17D.4.2 to 17D.5.1 - 1,500 rounds fired.	
	30/31	3.30am	A mine was got up in the top of Bull Sector, which was followed by heavy shelling for about one hour with shrapnel & heavy H.E. of the Support Line Flanken Road. Fire was opened with three guns traversing enemies support line from 10.D.4 to 17.6.5.0. - 3,750 rounds fired.	

J. Nisbet? Lt. M.G. Coy.

Confidential WAR DIARY or INTELLIGENCE SUMMARY
Army Form C. 2118.

Brigade Martins Gun Brigade
152nd Inf. Brigade

Place	Date	Hour	Summary of Events and Information	Remarks and references to Appendices
In the field	April 1916 1/4	1.30 pm	Headquarters of Company in Trenches A.15°D.0.5.13". (Reference — Bouleaumont 1:5,000. B.N.W.1. Ed. 2.B.1/1:10,000). Twelve guns in Trenches and four in Brigade Rooms at Maroeuil.	
	2nd	4.30 pm	A Camouflet was put up by us in sector left of the Brigade and indirect fire was opened with three guns in support trenches, 10D, 11D, 11D.17H and 17B. – 2,750 rounds fired. Indirect fire scheme with five guns on enemy's trenches. 11A.3.2.16. 11A.9.9. on junction of trenches. 17B.6.7 and 11D.7.3. on enemy's trenches. 11D.7.6.17C.4.4. on road 17D.7.0.6.17A.2.8. on enemy's trenches 17A.9.5.6. 18A.4.1. on junction of trenches. 11A.3.2. & 11A.9.9. 4,250 rounds fired.	
	2/3		Enemy aeroplane was brought down north of our aeroplanes. Indirect fire scheme with four guns on roads 17A.7.0.6.18A.2.8. and 17C.1.3.6.18A.2.8. on enemy's trenches 17A.7.5.6. 18A.4.9, 17C.9.2 to 17D.6.2, 10D.9.6. 11A.9.10. D.7.5.6.11B.3.3. 10D.0.9.6.11A.9.10.-4,500 rounds.	
	3/4		On wire being put up on Brigade sector on our left, carriage fire was opened on support lines. From 10D.6.9.6.17A.H.6 with 4 guns. 5,000 rounds.	
	4/5		Indirect fire scheme on Road. 17D.7.0.6.18A.2. Sand Road 18.C.6.3. to 18A.2.8. with two guns 3,000 rounds fired. 16 Sheppards reported that enemy replied with trench mortar at each burst of our fire.	
	5/6		Lewis gun support. Nothing to report.	
	6/7		Indirect fire scheme with two guns on enemy's trenches 17A.9.5.6 18A.4.1 and 17B.3.7.6.17D.10.8. 2,750 rounds fired.	

Confidential

WAR DIARY or INTELLIGENCE SUMMARY

Army Form C. 2118

Brigade Machine Gun Coy. 152nd Inf. Brigade

(Erase heading not required.)

Instructions regarding War Diaries and Intelligence Summaries are contained in F. S. Regs., Part II. and the Staff Manual respectively. Title Pages will be prepared in manuscript.

Place	Date	Hour	Summary of Events and Information	Remarks and references to Appendices
In the field	9/16			
	7/16	4 p.m.	Indirect fire scheme on map 17A.7.0 to 18A.2.8. two guns on 18C.6.3.6 - 18A.2.5. - 2,250 rounds fired.	
	8/16	9 —	Indirect fire scheme, cooperating with Artillery, according to "instructions received" Junction of Commn. trench 11.B.3.16 11.C.4.1. 17A.3.6 to 17B.6.7. 17C.5.2. to 17D.5.2., 17A.3.6. to 17A.4.6. and at junction 10 D.9.5. 5,000 rounds fired.	
	9/16	4 —	Quiet in support, nothing to report.	
	10/16	12 —	Indirect fire scheme on trenches 11 A.9.6, 11 A.7.6., 11 A.5.1.8.5. C.5.1. 1,000 rounds fired.	
	11/16	4 p.m.	Quiet in support; nothing to report.	
	12/16		" " " " " "	
	13/16	4 p.m.	Indirect fire scheme on tramway trench 17A.9.5. to 18A.0.5 and on C.4. 6.3 (2000 rounds)	
	14/16	4 p.m.	" with four guns on tramway trench 18.17A.6.5 to 18A.0.5 to 11 Capt. 6 and — on Commn. trench 17 A.6.5 to 18 A.2.8. 3,000 rounds fired.	
	14/16	11 —	" " on Tramway trench. 17 A.4.5. to 17B.4.5. 5,500 rounds fired.	
	15/16		Enemy replied a fresh burst of fire, with two rounds shrapnel in direction of Ypres.	
	15/16	4 p.m.	Indirect fire scheme on Trench junction, 11 A.5.4 + 17 A.6.4.5; and junction of trenches 11.D.7.3 and 11.C.4.2. — 2,000 rounds fired.	
	16/16	4 p.m.	Indirect fire scheme, cooperating with Artillery and French Mortars, also trenches 17 A.0.3. to 11 A.4.2 and 17 A.3.1. to 11 B.4.2. 1,300 rounds fired.	
	17/16	8 —	Indirect fire scheme, with four guns, in cooperation with 5th Rifle & 9 Coy. on tramway trench 17 B.7.5 to 17.C.4.6. and on trench 11 A.7.3.	

WAR DIARY ~~Confidential~~ Brigade Machine Gun Army Form C. 2118
or
INTELLIGENCE SUMMARY 152nd Inf. Brigade
(Erase heading not required.)

Instructions regarding War Diaries and Intelligence Summaries are contained in F.S. Regs., Part II. and the Staff Manual respectively. Title Pages will be prepared in manuscript.

Place	Date 1916	Hour	Summary of Events and Information	Remarks and references to Appendices
In the field	April 18/19	9 p.m. to 5 a.m.	Indirect fire scheme with two guns on Communt. Trenches, 11C.4.1 to 11D.2.6 and 11C.9.9 to 11D.9.0. on Support line 2.B.A.7.4 to 24.C.1.9. on Tramway Junctions 11A.34 to 11B.9.0 on Tramway Trench 11B.1 to 11D.2.6.	
	19/20	9 p.m. to 5 a.m.	Indirect fire scheme with two guns on Communt. Trench 11B.1 to 11D.2.6. on Tramway Trench 11A.5.4 to 11B.9.0 and 24.A.0.9. to 11A.8.8 and 17C.9.9.6.18.C.5.9. Four guns fired at intervals throughout night on trench junctions at: 11C.3.7, 10D.10.6, 11C.8.3, 11A.0.1.	
	20/21	9 p.m. to 2 a.m.	Indirect fire scheme on Communt. trenches 11D.7.2 to 12.C.2.3, 17A.7.4.5 to 17B.10.5: 17A.6.5 to 17.B.0.6, 17.D.4.2.6.24.A.1.9. — 2,500 rounds fired	
	21/22	9 p.m. to 2 a.m.	Indirect fire scheme on Avenues 17A.7.5, 6.18A.5.9, 10B.8.4. 6.5.C.8.4, 10D.7.8.6.5.D.1.6. 17A.7.5: 6.18A 4.9, 23A.7.4. to 24.C.1.9, 17C.9.2, 17C.9.9.6.17D.9.0 on Tramway trenches. 12.C.4.7.6.12.C.6.9, 17A.7.4.5 to 17B.10.5: — 6,500 rounds fired.	
	22/23	9 p.m. to 3 a.m.	Indirect fire scheme on Tramway Trench 17A.7.2 to 18.A.2.9, 17A.4.6 to 11D.6.3, 12.D.8.3.6.12.C.1.4. on Avenues 17A.7.5: 6.18.A.5.9.	
	23/24	9 p.m. to 4 a.m.	Indirect fire scheme cooperating with trench group artillery on Tramway Trench 12.C.3.7 to 12.C.9.8, out scheme on Avenues 10D.7.8.6.5.D.1.1. 17C.9.9 6.18.C.5.9. — 3,000 rounds fired.	
	24/25	9 p.m. to 3 a.m.	Indirect fire scheme on Avenues 17C.9.9.6.18.C.5.9. on Tramway Tracks 11A.5.11.6. 11B.9.0, 17A.7.5 6, 17.A.10.5; on Junctions of Avenues + Tramway + Tracks 11D.7.6.12.C. 2.5:- 2,000 rounds fired.	
	25/26	9 p.m. to ?	Quiet no support line nothing to report.	
	26/27	9 p.m. to ?	Indirect fire scheme in cooperation with left group artillery, on Trenches 10B.4.6.5.C.8.4. — 3,000 rounds fired. (152nd Batt. M.G.1.)	

WAR DIARY ~~or INTELLIGENCE SUMMARY~~

Army Form C. 2118.

Bugle Machine Gun Coy
162nd Inf. Brigade

Place	Date	Hour	Summary of Events and Information	Remarks and references to Appendices
OPPY In the field	28/4/17	2.45 / 7 pm	Enemy exploded mine in our front, and followed them by a very heavy bombardment along our front. Our guns from overhead positions immediately opened barrage fire on enemy's Supports and Communications. The enemy artillery barrage fell short of "Chemin Crent." Line by about 50 yards. 13,000 rounds fired.	
	26/4/17 27/4/17 29/30		Quiet in Support line, nothing to report. Indirect fire returned on Tramway Trench 17A 7.0 4.5. to 18A 0.5 on avenues 17A 7.5 to 18A 2.9 and on A.0.9 to 2H A5B - 4,000 rounds fired	Capt. Comi. 162nd Bde. M.G. Coy

J. Hundenfandr

Capt. Comi.
162nd
Bde. M.G. Coy

"Confidential"

War Diary
of
152nd Bde. M.G. Coy.

from 1st to 31st May. 1916.

[signature]

Captain,
O.C.,
152nd Inf. Bde. M.G. Coy.

Confidential

Brigade Machine Gun Army Form C. 2118.
152nd Inf Brigade

WAR DIARY
INTELLIGENCE SUMMARY
(Erase heading not required.)

Instructions regarding War Diaries and Intelligence Summaries are contained in F. S. Regs., Part II. and the Staff Manual respectively. Title Pages will be prepared in manuscript.

Place	Date 1916	Hour	Summary of Events and Information	Remarks and references to Appendices
In the field	Aug 1st/2nd		1st/2nd Headquarters of Company in Trenches A.15.D.a.5.15- (Reference Bochincourt - 57.B. N.W.1. Ed. 2.B. 1/10.000) Twelve guns in Trenches and four in Brigade Reserve at Maroeuil.	
			Buits in Support Line. Indirect fire exercises were carried out on enemy communication Trenches, Tramway Tracks and Roads.	
	20th		During heavy bombardment, further north in the evening the effect factory and tory shells fired in direction of batteries behind our lines was felt in the Reserve and Support Lines.	
			Six guns in support relieved by 154th Bde. M.G. Coy.	
	22nd		Relieved 154th Bde M.G. Coy. with six guns in support.	
	23rd		Six guns in support relieved by 154th Bde. M.G. Coy.	
	24th		Company Hqrs. moved to Maroeuil - leaving two guns in support.	
	25th		Two guns relieved by 153rd Bde M.G. Coy. and Company moved from Maroeuil to Aubigny.	
	26th/29th		In Rest Billets at Aubigny.	
	30th		Relieved six guns of 73rd Bde M.G. Coy. and two guns of 7th Bde. M.G. Coy in O. and P. Sectors. Remainder of Company in Aubigny.	
	31st		Relieved four guns of 7th Bde. M.G. Coy in P. Sector. Company HQrs. moved to Ecoivres. Four guns in Bde Reserve at Ecoivres.	

Winton Stubbs
Captain
O/C 152nd Bde Inf Coy.

"Confidential."

War Diary
of
152nd Bde. Machine Gun Coy.

from 1st to 30th June, 1916

A Bryd Captain,
for O.C.
152nd Bde. M.G. Coy.

"Confidential"

WAR DIARY 15:2nd Bttl. Machine Gun Coy. Army Form C. 2118.
or
INTELLIGENCE SUMMARY
(Erase heading not required.)

Instructions regarding War Diaries and Intelligence Summaries are contained in F. S. Regs., Part II. and the Staff Manual respectively. Title Pages will be prepared in manuscript.

Place	Date 1916	Hour	Summary of Events and Information	Remarks and references to Appendices
In the field	June 1st		Headquarters of Company in Neuville St. Vaast. Twelve Guns in trenches and four in Brigade Reserve at Ecoivres.	
	11th		Four Guns in Brigade Reserve at Ecoivres taken into Support at Neuville St. Vaast, making sixteen guns in trenches.	
	19th		Four guns in Neuville St. Vaast taken into Brigade Reserve at Ecoivres, making twelve in trenches and four in Brigade Reserve.	
	20th			
	25th		Four guns in Brigade Reserve Ecoivres taken into Support at Neuville St. Vaast, making sixteen guns in trenches.	
	27th			
	30th			

W. Wright Captain
O. C. C.
15-2nd Bttl. M.G. Coy.

152nd Brigade.
51st Division.

152nd BRIGADE MACHINE GUN COMPANY

JULY 1 9 1 6

152nd Inf. Brigade
SECRET No. 134.

WAR DIARY
of
152 Machine Gun Company.

July, 1916.

SECRET

WAR DIARY
INTELLIGENCE SUMMARY

Army Form C.2118.

152nd Brigade M.G. Coy.

Instructions regarding War Diaries and Intelligence Summaries are contained in F.S. Regs., Part II. and the Staff Manual respectively. Title Pages will be prepared in manuscript.

(Erase heading not required.)

Place	Date	Hour	Summary of Events and Information	Remarks and references to Appendices
In the field	1916			
	11th		Headquarters of Company in Neuville St. VAAST. Twelve guns in support and four in Brigade reserve at ECOIVRES	A
	12th		Company relieved by 50th Bde. M.G. Coy, and moved to ECOIVRES.	A
	13th		" moved to billets at ACQ.	A
	14th		" in rest billets at ACQ	A
	15th		" moved to billets at BOUDRINCOURT by motor transport	A
	16th		" " " LONGVILLETTE	A
	17th		" in rest billets at LONGVILLETTE	A
	18th		" " " " "	A
	19th		" " " " "	A
	20th		Transport moved to BUIRE. Company moved by train from CANDAS to MERRICOURT, and marched to BUIRE.	A
	21st		Company moved to bivouacs at eastern edge of FRICOURT WOOD. X.29.	A
	22nd		Heavily shelled in the afternoon. One OR slightly wounded.	A
	23rd		Company moved to bivouacs near FRICOURT, at F.2.	A
	24th		" " " BECORDEL - BECOURT.	A

SECRET.

WAR DIARY 15-2nd Bde M.G. Coy
or
INTELLIGENCE SUMMARY

Army Form C. 2118.

Place	Date 1916	Hour	Summary of Events and Information	Remarks and references to Appendices
In the field July	26th		Company less transport, with sixteen guns moved up to eastern edge of MAMETZ WOOD at S. 20. A.O.O. Transport lines near BECORDEL-BECOURT Shelters taken over were very poor. During the night shelled heavily with gas shells. Casualties one O.R. killed (Gas), and six O.R. wounded (Gas).	
	27th		Casualties from shelling in 26th. Two more O.R. wounded (Gas) ʃ	
	28th		" " " " " Two " " " (") ʃ	
	29th		Transport lines moved to near FRICOURT at F.2 Company in shelters at eastern edge of MAMETZ WOOD S. 20. A.O.O. Shelled in afternoon. Casualties one O.R. Shell Shock	ʃ
	30th		Heavily shelled in afternoon. Casualties 2nd Lieut Archer no wounded One O.R. killed. Three O.R. Wounded.	ʃ
	31st		Company in shelters at eastern edge of MAMETZ WOOD S. 20. A.O.O.	

W. Emsley 2nd Lieut
for OC
15-2nd Bde. M.G. Coy

152nd Brigade
51st Division.

152nd BRIGADE MACHINE GUN COMPANY

AUGUST 1 9 1 6 ::::

Secret.

WAR DIARY

152nd Machine Gun Coy.

Army Form C. 2118.

INTELLIGENCE SUMMARY

CONFIDENTIAL
No. 21 (A)
HIGHLAND DIVISION

Instructions regarding War Diaries and Intelligence Summaries are contained in F.S. Regs., Part II. and the Staff Manual respectively. Title Pages will be prepared in manuscript.

(Erase heading not required.)

Place	Date	Hour	Summary of Events and Information	Remarks and references to Appendices
In the field	1/8/16		Relieved the 153rd Machine Gun Company with four guns in support and four guns in reserve at MAMETZ WOOD. Reserve section were heavily shelled in the morning for two hours.	A
	2/8/16		Quiet all day.	A
	3/8/16		Shoots in HIGH WOOD shelled heavily in the morning. Indirect barrage scheme with four guns complete. Indirect fire scheme carried out on Switch trench & on tracks & roads behind HIGH WOOD	A
	4/8/16		Indirect fire scheme carried out on enemy tracks behind HIGH WOOD & on Switch trench	A
	5/8/16		Indirect fire scheme carried out cooperating with Lewis Guns & trench mortars on roads & tracks behind HIGH WOOD.	A
	6/8/16		Indirect fire scheme carried out on full gun positions where guns observed firing in front of MARTINPUICH.	A
	7/8/16		Company relieved by 100th Machine Gun Company & moved into bivouacs near BUIRE	A
	8/8/16		Transport of Company moved to CARDONETTE.	A

Army Form C. 2118.

WAR DIARY
INTELLIGENCE SUMMARY

2 Revd. 15-2nd Machine Gun Coy.

(Erase heading not required.)

Instructions regarding War Diaries and Intelligence Summaries are contained in F. S. Regs., Part II. and the Staff Manual respectively. Title Pages will be prepared in manuscript.

Place	Date	Hour	Summary of Events and Information	Remarks and references to Appendices
In the field	9.8.16		Company less transport moved by train from MERICOURT to LONGPRE. Transport move by road from CARDONETTE to LONGPRE.	A
	9/8/16 11		Company billetted in LONGPRE.	A
	11.8.16		Company entrained at LONGPRE for THIENNES via HAZEBROUCK	A
	12.8.16		Company detrained at THIENNES & moved to Billets at LECROQUET near BLARINGHAM.	A
	12.8.16 /18		Company billetted in LECROQUET.	A
	18.8.16		Transport moved by road to ARMENTIERES and remainder of Company by rail from EBBLINGHEM to STEENWERCKE and thence by road to ARMENTIERES.	A
	18/8/16 26		Brigade in Divisional Reserve. Company billetted in ARMENTIERES and transport three miles out of town	A
	26.8.16		Company relieved the 154th Machine Gun Company in right Sector with three guns in front line & nine guns in support & form	A

WAR DIARY 15-2nd Machine Gun Coy
INTELLIGENCE SUMMARY

Army Form C. 2118.

Place	Date	Hour	Summary of Events and Information	Remarks and references to Appendices
La Chapelle	26.8.16		Guns in Brigade Reserve in ARMENTIERES. Headquarters of Company at LA CHAPELLE D'ARMENTIERES.	A
	29.8.16 5.30		Quiet on the line. Indirect fire schemes were carried out on enemy trenches & roads.	A
	31.8.16		Company guns co-operate in fire scheme against enemy trenches, trench roads & strong points.	A

Windon Fawkes Capt
Comdg 152nd Machine Gun Company

Headquarters,
    152nd Inf. Brigade.
    ------- - ---

I send herewith War Diary for August, 1916, for unit under my Command.

[signature]

                                            Capt.
                                Comdg. 152nd Co. M.G. Corps.

5. 9. 16.

SECRET
No. 134
152nd INF. BDE.

WAR   DIARY
of
152nd MACHINE GUN COMPANY.

From
1st September, 1916
To
30th September, 1916.
****

Secret

Army Form C. 2118.

WAR DIARY
or
INTELLIGENCE SUMMARY

152ⁿᵈ /16ᵗʰ Machine Gun Coy

(Erase heading not required.)

Place	Date	Hour	Summary of Events and Information	Remarks and references to Appendices
Field	1.9.16		Company in Right Sector ARMENTIERES with three guns in front line, nine in support & supporting points and four in Brigade Reserve in ARMENTIERES.	A
	2/3/9/16		Indirect fire schemes were carried out on enemy roads tracks tramway tracks & trenches.	A
	3.9.16		One gun in front line moved into supporting point making two guns in front line, ten guns in support & supporting points and four guns in Brigade Reserve.	A
	4.9.16		Indirect fire schemes carried out on enemy front line trenches in cooperation with Mortars.	A
	5.9.16		Indirect fire schemes carried out in cooperation with Artillery on enemy roads tracks & trenches	A

W. MacAnn

Army Form C. 2118.

WAR DIARY or INTELLIGENCE SUMMARY

152nd Machine Gun Coy.

(Erase heading not required.)

Place	Date	Hour	Summary of Events and Information	Remarks and references to Appendices
Trin.	6/8 9/9/16		Instruct the scheme now carried out on enemy roads & tracks and trenches.	A
"	9/9/16		In cooperation with 102nd Machine Gun Coy & with artillery indirect fire schemes were carried out on enemy roads tracks and trenches	A
"	10/12 9/9/16		Indirect fire schemes were carried out on enemy roads tracks and trenches.	A
"	13/14 9/9/16		Fired the schemes in cooperation with Artillery & Trench Mortars on enemy roads tracks & fixed lines trenches. Bursts of fire during night on Railway line trenches, enemy working parties & trenches & roads during the day by fixed Trench Mortars.	A
"	15/9/16		Cooperation with "barrage" fire by thirteen guns covering advance of 6th Seaforth Hghrs & 6nd Gordon Hghrs. Reinforced line Z 95 60.	A

W.A. Ainslie Major

Army Form C. 2118.

WAR DIARY
or
INTELLIGENCE SUMMARY

153rd Machine Gun Company

(Erase heading not required.)

Place	Date	Hour	Summary of Events and Information	Remarks and references to Appendices
Sus	16.9.16		Cooperated with four guns in connection with raid by 154th Inft. Bde. from the frontage of 152nd Inft. Bn. Indirect fire schemes were carried out on enemy roads, tracks and trenches.	A
	17.9.16			
	18.9.16		In every relief long indirect fire schemes were carried on enemy roads tracks & trenches. Rounds fired 17500.	A
	19.9.16		The Company was relieved by the 153rd Machine Gun Coy & moved to training Camp under canvas at S 27 b. 15 miles S.E. of BAILLEUL	A
	20.9.16		Company in training Camp at S 27 b.	A
	21.9.16		Four Guns and personnel moved to Billets at ARMENTIERES to cooperate in raid by 6th Gordon Highrs on the night of 22nd/23rd.	A
	22.9.16		Remainder of Company in training Camp at S 27 b. M.H.Andrews Major	A

2449 Wt. W14957/M90 750,000 1/16 J.B.C. & A. Forms/C.2118/12.

Army Form C. 2118.

WAR DIARY
or
INTELLIGENCE SUMMARY

Strict. 152nd Machine Gun Coy.

(Erase heading not required.)

Place	Date	Hour	Summary of Events and Information	Remarks and references to Appendices
Hth.	23.9.16		Cooperated in raid by 6th Gordon Highrs on enemy thrown out salient with two guns firing barrage fire. 17000 rounds fired. Guns & personnel returned to Training Camp S.27.b.	A
"	24/31 9/16		Company in Training Camp S.27.b. under canvas carrying out training programme.	A
"	31.9.16		Company entrained at Bailleul & detrained at Doullens and moved to Billets at Longuilette.	A

W. Smith
Major.

WAR DIARY
of
152nd COMPANY, MACHINE GUN CORPS.

From
1st October, 1916.
To
31st October, 1916.

Secret.

WAR DIARY
or
INTELLIGENCE SUMMARY

152nd Machine Gun Company

Army Form C. 2118.

No 2-/A/

HIGHLAND DIVISION.

Place	Date	Hour	Summary of Events and Information	Remarks and references to Appendices
	1·10·16		Company billeted in LONGUEVILLETTE.	A
	2·10·16		Company moved by road to bivouacs in BOIS DE WARNIMONT near AUTHIE	A
	3·10·16		Company in bivouacs in BOIS DE WARNIMONT.	A
	4·10·16		Relieved the 6th Machine Gun Company & 99th Machine Gun Company in sector South of HEBUTERNE. Two guns in support and supporting positions and seven guns in reserve in HEBUTERNE	A
	5·6·7·10·16		Nothing to report	A
	7·10·16		Two guns in left subsector relieved by the 56th Machine Gun Coy and three guns in left subsector relieved by the 58th Machine Gun Coy. Headquarters of Company moved to COIGNEUX with four guns in support and twelve in reserve in COIGNEUX.	A
	8·10·16 9th/11th /10/16		Company relieved by 154th Company & moved into billets at LOUVENCOURT.	A
			In billets at LOUVENCOURT.	
	12·10·16 13th/ /16 /10/16		Company moved into bivouacs at BUS LES ARTOIS	A
			In bivouacs at BUS LES ARTOIS	
	14·10·16		Relieved the 116th Company in AUCHONVILLERS sector with ten guns in support, two guns in reserve in AUCHONVILLERS and four in reserve in MAILLY-MAILLET wood.	A

WAR DIARY or INTELLIGENCE SUMMARY

Army Form C. 2118.

152nd Machine Gun Company

(Erase heading not required.)

Place	Date	Hour	Summary of Events and Information	Remarks and references to Appendices
Huon	18/19/20/10/16		Indirect fire schemes were carried out on enemy trenches and roads in BEAUMONT-HAMEL.	A
	21.10.16		Guns cooperated with artillery in connection with operations south of Serre. Four guns in right subsector were relieved by the 153rd Coy having one gun in support, two in reserve in AUCHONVILLERS and two with A Company in reserve in MAILLY-MAILLET wood.	A
	22.10.16		Company relieved by 154th Company & moved to huts at HEAUVILLERS.	A
	23.10.16		Moved to huenues at P19 c 5.2	A
	24.20/10/16		In huenues at P19 c 5.2	A
	29.10.16		Four guns placed in right subsector to unfilade German wire	A
	30.10.16		Company relieved 154th Company. Four guns in support in right subsector, two guns in support in left subsector, two guns in reserve in AUCHONVILLERS and four guns in reserve in P19 c 5.2	A
	30 & 31/10/16		During hours of darkness our guns fired on enemy front line wire & supporting trenches.	A
	31.10.16		During the night firing guns in night subsector were heavily shelled.	A

Signed _____
152nd Machine Gun Company

WAR DIARY

of
152nd COMPANY, MACHINE GUN CORPS.

NOVEMBER, 1916.

Army Form C. 2118.

WAR DIARY
or
INTELLIGENCE SUMMARY

(Erase heading not required.)

Instructions regarding War Diaries and Intelligence Summaries are contained in F. S. Regs., Part II. and the Staff Manual respectively. Title Pages will be prepared in manuscript.

Place	Date	Hour	Summary of Events and Information	Remarks and references to Appendices
In the Field	1/11 to 4/11		10 guns in Support in BEAUMONT Sectn, 2 guns in Reserve in AUCHONVILLERS, 4 guns in Reserve at P.17.d. Night firing schemes carried out on enemy lines.	Nun.
	5/11		6 guns in Support and 2 guns at AUCHONVILLERS relieved by 154 M.G.Coy, and moved back to P.17.d. Nightfiring schemes on enemy lines carried out by remaining 4 guns.	Nun.
	6/11		12 guns at P.17.d. moved to billets at FORCEVILLE.	Nun.
	7/11 to 11/11		12 guns in billets at FORCEVILLE. Night firing schemes carried out by 4 guns in line.	Nun.
	12/11		Relieved 154 M.G.Coy in BEAUMONT Sectn preparatory to attack. 16 guns in line.	Nun.
	13/11		ATTACK on BEAUMONT. 4 guns took up positions in German front line immediately it was consolidated. 8/1 guns accompanied infantry in captured trenches. 12 guns were employed barrage fire during attack. Night firing schemes carried out during afternoon and evening.	Nun.
	14/11		12 guns in captured trenches. 4 guns in reserve in old British Support line. Indirect fire schemes carried out.	Nun.
	15/11 16/11		Coy relieved by 154 M.G.Coy, and moved back to bivouacs in MAILLY WOOD.	Nun.
	17/11 18/11		In bivouacs in MAILLY WOOD.	Nun.
	19/11		Relieved 6 guns of 182 M.G.Coy in front line BEAUMONT Sectn. Established 6 other guns in Support position. Remaining 4 guns in MAILLY WOOD.	Nun.
	20/11 23/11		12 guns in line. 4 guns in Reserve in MAILLY WOOD. Indirect fire schemes carried out.	Nun.
	24/11		Relieved by 91st M.G.Coy. Moved to billets in FORCEVILLE.	Nun.
	25/11 26/11		In billets at FORCEVILLE.	Nun.
	27/11		Moved to billets at BOUZINCOURT.	Nun.
	28/11 30/11		In billets at BOUZINCOURT.	Nun.

A. Withers Lieut.
for Major Commanding
152 MGCoy.
30.xi.16.

WAR DIARY

of

152nd COMPANY, MACHINE GUN CORPS.

From

1st December, 1916.

To

31st December, 1916.

Army Form C. 2118.

WAR DIARY
or
INTELLIGENCE SUMMARY
(Erase heading not required.)

Instructions regarding War Diaries and Intelligence Summaries are contained in F. S. Regs., Part II. and the Staff Manual respectively. Title Pages will be prepared in manuscript.

Place	Date	Hour	Summary of Events and Information	Remarks and references to Appendices
In the Field	1 Decr. to 3 Decr.		In billets at BOUZINCOURT. (Brigade in Reserve).	Firing.
	4 Decr.		Moved to huts at OVILLERS POST. (Brigade in Support).	Firing.
	8 Decr. 9 Decr.		Relieved 154 M.G.Coy. in the Line – 6 guns in support, 6 guns on indirect barrage fire, 2 guns in reserve at Adv. H.Q. (R.29.c.55.) and 2 guns in reserve at Rear H.Q. (OVILLERS POST)	Firing.
	9 Decr. to 13 Decr.		In the Line. Indirect firing on selected points behind enemy lines.	Firing. Firing.
	14 Decr. 15 Decr.		Relieved by 153 M.G.Coy. and moved to huts at OVILLERS POST.	Firing.
	16 Decr.		Relieved by 154 M.G.Coy and moved to billets at BOUZINCOURT.	Firing.
	17 Decr. to 22 Decr.		In billets at BOUZINCOURT.	Firing.
	22 Decr.		Moved to huts at OVILLERS POST.	
	26 Decr. 27 Decr.		Relieved 154 M.G.Coy in the Line – 7 guns in support, 5 guns on indirect barrage fire, 2 guns in reserve at Adv. H.Q. and 2 guns in reserve at Rear H.Q.	Firing.
	27 Decr. to 31 Decr.		In the Line. Indirect firing on selected points behind enemy lines.	Firing.

1 January 1917.

Hunables
Lieut.
for Major Commanding
152 Machine Gun Coy.

152nd Inf. Bde. SECRET No. 134

W A R   D I A R Y
of
152nd COMPANY, MACHINE GUN CORPS.

CONFIDENTIAL.
No 21 (A)
HIGHLAND
DIVISION.

FROM
1st JANUARY, 1917
TO
31st JANUARY, 1917.

Army Form C. 2118.

WAR DIARY
or
INTELLIGENCE SUMMARY
(Erase heading not required.)

CONFIDENTIAL
No 719
HIGHLAND DIVISION.

Instructions regarding War Diaries and Intelligence Summaries are contained in F.S. Regs, Part II. and the Staff Manual respectively. Title Pages will be prepared in manuscript.

Place	Date	Hour	Summary of Events and Information	Remarks and references to Appendices
In the Field	1/1/17		Company in the line COURCELETTE SECTOR. 7 guns in Support positions. 5 in barrage positions. 2 in reserve at Adv. H.Q. and 2 in reserve at Rear H.Q.	From
	2/1/17		Relieved by 153 M.G. Coy and moved into 6 DUILLERS HUTS.	From
	3/1/17		Moved to billets at BOUZINCOURT.	From
	9/1/17		Relieved 154 M.G. Coy in DUILLERS HUTS.	From
	12/1/17		Moved to billets at BOUZINCOURT.	From
	13/1/17		Moved to BEAUQUESNE by march route.	From
	14/1/17		" GRIMONT " " "	From
	15/1/17		" HANCHY " " "	From
	16/1/17		" NOUVION EN PONTHIED " "	From
	17/1/17 to 31/1/17		Instructional and Recreational training at NOUVION.	From

Lundiken
Lieut
for Main Commanding
152 Machine Gun Coy.

SECRET
No. 134
152nd INF. BDE.

WAR DIARY

of

152nd MACHINE GUN COMPANY

from

1st FEBRUARY 1917.

to

28th FEBRUARY 1917.

Army Form C. 2118.

WAR DIARY
or
INTELLIGENCE SUMMARY

(Erase heading not required.)

Instructions regarding War Diaries and Intelligence Summaries are contained in F. S. Regs., Part II. and the Staff Manual respectively. Title Pages will be prepared in manuscript.

SECRET

Place	Date	Hour	Summary of Events and Information	Remarks and references to Appendices
In the Field	1917			
	1 Feb – 4 Feb		In billets at NOUVION EN PONTHIEU Training.	him.
	5 Feb.		Moved by march route to MAISON PONTHIEU.	him.
	6 "		" " " " ISACHIMONT.	him.
	7 "		" " " " GUINECOURT.	him.
	8 "		" " " " MONCHY BRETON.	him.
	9 "		" " " " ACQ.	him.
	10 "		Relieved 26th M.G.C. (11 guns) and 27th M.G.C. (5 guns) in the line – ROCLINCOURT SECTOR. Rear H.Q. at ANZIN and Transport at MARŒUIL.	him.
	11 Feb – 26 Feb		In the line. Harrassing fire schemes carried out on enemy trenches and lines of approach.	him.
	27 Feb.		Relieved by 154 M.G.C. and moved to billets at ACQ.	him.
	28 Feb		In billets at ACQ.	him.

Andrews.
Lieut.
for Major Commanding
152 Machine Gun Coy.

28 February 1917.

SECRET
No. 134
152nd INF. BDE.

Vol 15

WAR DIARY.

of

152nd MACHINE GUN COMPANY.

From

1st MARCH, 1917.

to

31st MARCH, 1917.

WAR DIARY
INTELLIGENCE SUMMARY

Army Form C. 2118.

152nd Company M.G.C.

Place	Date	Hour	Summary of Events and Information	Remarks and references to Appendices
Maroeuil	1.3.17		Company in Billets at M.C.Q.	A
	2.3.17		to move to Billets at MAROEUIL.	A
	4.3.17		Eight guns and personnel moved to line ROCLINCOURT for raid of 1/6th Gordon Highrs. Eight guns remaining at MAROEUIL.	A
	5.3.17 6 am		Eight guns cooperated in covering flanks of raiding party of 1/6 Gordon Highrs. 28,750 rounds fired.	A
	6.3.17		Eight guns returned to MAROEUIL after the raid.	A
	12.3.17		Company moved to Billets at CAUCOURT	
	14.3.17		Six guns moved to CACQ and two guns to FREVIN CAPELLE for anti-aircraft duty at Dumps.	A
	16.3.17		Eight guns moved to MAROEUIL.	A
	17.3.17 6 am		Eight guns moved to line ROCLINCOURT for raid of 1/8th Arg. & Suth. Highrs. 1st & 1/5th & 1/8th guns cooperated in covering flanks of raiding party of 1/8th Arg. & Suth. Highrs. 17,000 rounds fired. Eight guns moved to CAUCOURT after raid.	A
	22.3.17		Eight guns ( ) and H.Q. & and Transport moved to Hurts, ECOIVRES	A
	23.3.17		One officer & 40 other ranks moved into line to carry out work on emplacements & shelters for operations.	A
	29.3.17		Guns at M.C.Q. relieved by guns & teams of 1/8th & Royal Scots, and joined Company at Hurts, ECOIVRES	A
	29.3.17		One officer & 6 2 other ranks on working party at MAROEUIL.	A
	30.3.17		Company billeted at Hurts, ECOIVRES. Two officers & 100 other ranks on working party at MAROEUIL.	A

W.A. Arbre Major

WAR DIARY

of

152nd MACHINE GUN COMPANY

for

APRIL, 1917.

WAR DIARY
or
INTELLIGENCE SUMMARY

Army Form C. 2118.

15 - 2ⁿᵈ Machine Gun Coy

Place	Date	Hour	Summary of Events and Information	Remarks and references to Appendices
In the field	1-4-17		Company billeted at X.H. hts. ECOIVRES. Party of Officers & N.C.O's. in the line, ROCLINCOURT SECTOR, preparing positions for attack.	A
	2.4.17		Two guns of Company relieved two guns of 153ʳᵈ Coy in the line in Right Subsector ROCLINCOURT.	A
	8.4.17		Company moved into assembly position for the attack on 9/4/17. H.Q'rs of Coy at Brigade H.Q'rs in ROCLINCOURT. Echelon 'B' moved to tanks at Bois de - BRAY.	A
	9.4.17		Attack on VIMY - ARRAS front - The Brigade frontage was:- A 23. C. 9. 3½. A.3. a. 2.3, Ref. ROCLINCOURT sheet 51.B.N.W. - The objectives of the attack were:- Black Line objective.- A.2.4.a.0.0./A.30.B.4.8. Blue Line -do- : A.24.a.5.6/B.19.&5.1. Brown Line -do- : B.14.c.6.2/B.20.d.6.1. The guns of the 15-2ⁿᵈ M.G. Coy, were employed as follows:- Four guns under Divisional arrangement, fired covering barrage for attack of Infantry, and on completion of barrage, were available for consolidation of lines captured and Reserve. Four Lewis guns were detailed for objectives, for consolidation of lines and four guns were detailed for Reserve.	A

Army Form C. 2118.

WAR DIARY

INTELLIGENCE SUMMARY

Army Form C. 2118.

153rd Machine Gun Coy

Place	Date	Hour	Summary of Events and Information	Remarks and references to Appendices
In the field	9.4.17		The objectives of the 12 guns were:- 2 guns in BLACK LINE at A.30.a.9.6., 2 guns in front between BLACK LINE and BLUE LINE at A.24.b.3.1., 4 guns in BLUE LINE, 2 at B.19.C.5.2. and 2 guns at B.24.b.7.4., 4 guns in STRONG POINTS between BLUE LINE and BROWN LINE, 2 guns in vicinity of B.19.d.5.9., and 2 guns in vicinity of B.19.d.3.9. - One Gun was put out of action during barrage. - Two guns moved for BLACK LINE at 6.42 a.m. and reached objective without casualties. The attack on the BLUE LINE was held up for some time by machine gun fire. - On the capture of Blue Line left subsector of BLUE LINE, 2 guns moved at 2.30 p.m. for STRONG POINT at A.24.b.3.1., 2 guns for BLUE LINE at B.24.b.7.4. and 2 guns for STRONG POINT at B.19.b.3.9. and reached objective without casualties. On the capture of Brigade Right subsector of BLUE LINE, 2 guns moved at 3 p.m. for BLUE LINE at B.19.C.5.2. and reached objective without casualties and 2 guns for STRONG POINTS in vicinity of B.24.b.7.4. positions were consolidated at front. B.19.d.3.3. for these guns; no troops were not then formed of this line guns were left in Brigade Reserve.	

WAR DIARY / INTELLIGENCE SUMMARY

Army Form C. 2118.

152nd Machine Gun Coy

Place	Date	Hour	Summary of Events and Information	Remarks and references to Appendices
In the field	9.4.17		The six guns in BLUE LINE were laid on a barrage, covering BROWN LINE and fired continuously during the night of 9th/10th.	
	10.4.17		An attack on the BROWN LINE which had not been captured, was ordered for 5 a.m. The six guns on BARRAGE, carried out intense barrage covering advance, from 5:30 a.m. to 6 a.m. The HQ. & "C" Company moved from ROCLINCOURT to BLACK LINE at A.24.c.7.3. Two guns in the BLACK LINE moved and three guns in RESERVE moved into BLUE LINE, making 11 guns for protective barrage - a protective barrage over BROWN LINE, was carried out during the hours of darkness. About 8 p.m., an S.O.S. was put up on left of 34th Division. Our immediate right and 4 guns firing an barrage line in front of MAISON de la COTE intensified their fire until the position quietened down. Echelon "B" moved to SANTY.	
	11.4.17		An attack on the BROWN LINE from B.20.a.7.4. to B.14.a.2.7. at 6.30 p.m. was ordered and a covering barrage scheme was arranged for the 11 guns of company. But the line was captured before 6.30 p.m. - The company was relieved on the night 11/12 by the 57th M.G. Coy. and 99th M.G. Coy. - Total casualties during operation:- 3 O.R. Killed - 1 O.R. Wounded	

Army Form C. 2118.

WAR DIARY
or
INTELLIGENCE SUMMARY.
(Erase heading not required.)

(H)

Place	Date	Hour	Summary of Events and Information	Remarks and references to Appendices
Fosseux	12.4.17		On relief the Company moved to "X" Huts, ECOIVRES	A
	13.4.17		Company moved to Villers at Tilloy	A
	16.4.17		———— to ———— ARRAS, by bus.	A
	17.4.17		Company moved to line in RAMPOUX sector, to prepare positions for our attack, expected on 20th April, 1917. 8 & Adv. B. at ARRAS 15·3·T. My Coy in the line.	A
	20.4.17		6 guns relieved 6 guns of 15·3·T. My Coy in the line.	
	22.4.17		Two guns of company put out of action — Company assembled in battle positions for the attack on 23rd April 17. H.Q. 23, of Coy. at H.23. b.3.1. – The Division Headquarters:– H.12. c. H.8.6. The SCARPE. Ref. RAMPOUX, 51.B. N.W.4. – The objectives of the attack were:– BLACK LINE. – H.12. A.9.9/ I.75. A.0.7. BLUE and BROWN LINES. I.8.d.1.5/ I.20.C.6.7. RED LINE. I.9.c.7.4/ I.21.a.0.1. The guns of the company were employed as follows:– 14 guns under Divisional arrangements from Barrage scheme covering advance of Infantry to the BLACK LINE, and 7 guns continued barrage scheme covering advance of the Infantry to the BLUE LINE, and then fell into Divisional Reserve. Two guns were out of action on completion of scheme, leaving 5 guns in Divisional Reserve.	A (5)

WAR DIARY

INTELLIGENCE SUMMARY.

152nd Machine Gun Coy.

Place	Date	Hour	Summary of Events and Information	Remarks and references to Appendices
In the field	March 17		On completion of barrage covering advance to Black Line, 3 guns moved for Black Line at I.19.a.8.7 to give covering fire in advance to RED LINE and then moved into BLUE LINE at I.14.C.0.6. and Cuyd. on protective barrage for RED LINE and 4 guns moved for BLUE LINE to give covering fire in advance to RED LINE. On arriving at our FRONT LINE, it was found that the BLACK LINE had not been taken and the advance to the BLACK LINE was held up until late in the forenoon. On the capture of BLACK LINE the 7 guns were moved into the line, and consolidated positions, then at 4 p.m. in the afternoon a line of posts were established 50/100 yards in advance of the CHEMICAL WORKS to the CEMETERY. Three guns were advanced behind line of posts to position at CHATEAM, I.13.d.1.1. and later 4 guns about 2/300 yards NORTH of CHATEAM. During the evening the vicinity of the CHEMICAL WORKS was heavily shelled. The section on the NORTH of CHATEAM suffered heavily and the four guns were buried and not recoverable.	6

Army Form C. 2118.

WAR DIARY
or
INTELLIGENCE SUMMARY. 15-2nd Machine Gun Coy

(Erase heading not required.)

Place	Date	Hour	Summary of Events and Information	Remarks and references to Appendices
In the field	23/4/17		Between 8. and 9. a.m. the enemy attacked, in strength, from ROEUX and surrounded the three gun detachments: 2 officers and 28 o.ranks are missing, including a number of wounded.	
	24/4/17 p.m.		The Company was relieved on the arrival of the 103rd M.G. Coy.	
	26/4/17		to relieve the 154th Coy. and moved into billets in ATHIES.	
	28/4/17 30/4/17		Company moved by bus to FREVIN-CAPELLE. Company moved to billets at MONCHEAUX.	

M.A. Ando
Major Comdg:
15-2nd Machine Gun Coy

WAR DIARY
of
152nd COMPANY, MACHINE GUN CORPS.

MAY, 1917.

SECRET

Instructions regarding War Diaries and Intelligence Summaries are contained in F.S. Regs, Part II. and the Staff Manual respectively. Title pages will be prepared in manuscript.

Army Form C. 2118.

WAR DIARY
or
INTELLIGENCE SUMMARY.
(Erase heading not required.)

152ND COMPANY
MACHINE GUN
CORPS.

Date 8/6/17

Place	Date	Hour	Summary of Events and Information	Remarks and references to Appendices
In the Field	1 May / 9 May	—	In billets at MONCHEAUX. Training and refitting	Nmn.
	10 May	—	Moved to ARRAS by Light Rail. Transport by road, and occupied billets in RUE DES AUGUSTINES and RUE DUFOURS ST. ADRIEN.	Nmn.
	12 May	—	Relieved 10th Machine Gun Company in the line, immediately S of Railway E of FAMPOUX. All guns up. Coy H.Q. established at ST. NICHOLAS.	Nmn.
	15 May	—	All positions heavily bombarded by enemy throughout the day. Enemy attack expected. Barrage scheme for seven guns in a reserve trench carried out at dusk. Strong barrier to neutralise the causalities throughout these fire fairly heavy — one gun knocked out.	Nmn.
	16 May	—	Enemy attacked at dawn. Barrage scheme immediately brought into operation. Two guns on left flank of Coy's Section together with two guns on support flank of Left Coy's Section captured by the enemy who broke through the front line system at this point — ie. along line of Railway. Subsequently one of these guns was found with the team lying around dead, the gun being badly handled and with a partially emptied belt. The infantry immediately committed and drove the enemy back, eventually arriving to line only a few yards in rear of our original front line. Also retaining the situation. All other guns in the	Map showing approx. positions attached.

WAR DIARY
or
INTELLIGENCE SUMMARY.

(Erase heading not required.)

Instructions regarding War Diaries and Intelligence Summaries are contained in F. S. Regs., Part II. and the Staff Manual respectively. Title pages will be prepared in manuscript.

Army Form C. 2118.

162ND COMPANY
MACHINE GUN
CORPS.
No............ 3/6/17

Place	Date	Hour	Summary of Events and Information	Remarks and references to Appendices
In the Field			Front line enemy held on and inflicted heavy casualties on the enemy. It is thought that the barrage was also very effective. Apart from the loss of the two guns on the left casualties this day were not exceptionally heavy. One other gun was knocked out by shell fire. Total casualties for the four days - 1 Officer killed, 2 Officers wounded, 6 O.R. killed, 20 O.R. wounded, 3 O.R. missing.	Arras
	17 May		14 guns in line relieved by 151st Machine Gun Coy. and moved back to billets in ARRAS in early morning. 2 remaining guns which were in support positions relieved at dusk.	Arras
	18 May – 23 May		In billets in ARRAS refitting.	
	24 May		Relieved 153rd Machine Gun Company in the line immediately N. of Railway E. of FAMPOUX. 1 Section kept in ARRAS in mobile reserve ready to be rushed up in motor lorries.	Arras
	25 May – 30 May		Positions heavily shelled by enemy but no attack eventuated - 1 Officer wounded, 4 O.R. killed, 7 O.R. wounded. One gun destroyed by shell fire. Reliefs were badly knocked about and there were practically no reliefs. Internal reliefs were carried out as necessity arose at irregular intervals.	Arras

SECRET

Army Form C. 2118.

152ND COMPANY,
MACHINE GUN
CORPS.
No ....
Date 3/6/17

WAR DIARY
or
INTELLIGENCE SUMMARY.
(Erase heading not required.)

Instructions regarding War Diaries and Intelligence Summaries are contained in F. S. Regs., Part II. and the Staff Manual respectively. Title pages will be prepared in manuscript.

Place	Date	Hour	Summary of Events and Information	Remarks and references to Appendices
In the Field	3/May	—	Relieved minor optimum and manning by 27th Machine Gun Co. and moved back to billets in ARRAS.	

Kunikers
Lieut.
Commanding 152 Mach. Gun Coy.

3 June 1917.

152ND COMPANY,
MACHINE GUN
CORPS.

SECRET

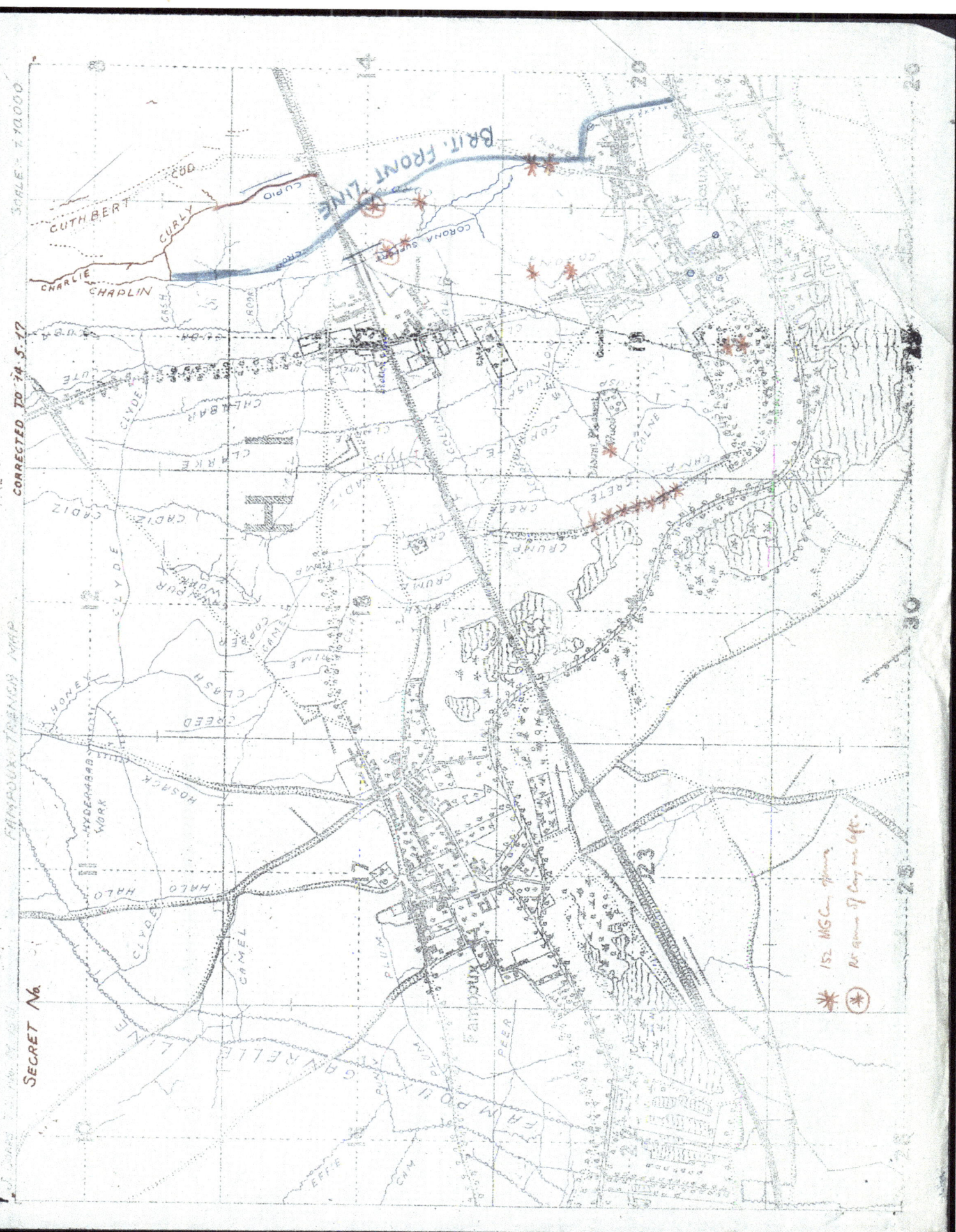

152ND COMPANY,
MACHINE GUN
CORPS.

No. 3/6/17

SECRET

WAR DIARY
of
152nd COMPANY, MACHINE GUN CORPS.

JUNE, 1917.

Army Form C. 2118.

WAR DIARY

INTELLIGENCE SUMMARY.

(Erase heading not required.)

Instructions regarding War Diaries and Intelligence Summaries are contained in F. S. Regs., Part II. and the Staff Manual respectively. Title pages will be prepared in manuscript.

Place	Date	Hour	Summary of Events and Information	Remarks and references to Appendices
	1.6.17		Company in billets at ARRAS	
	"	3am	Transport moved to TACHINCOURT	
	"	12noon	Company moved by tactical train to LIGNY ST FLOCHEL and then marched to TACHINCOURT.	A
	4.6.17	6.15AM	Company moved to Billets at BERGUENEUSE.	A
	5.6.17	9.30am	" " " " Coyecque.	A
	8.6.17	4am	" " " " St Croix (LONGUENESSE).	A
	9.6.17	4am	" " " " La Commune	A
	10.6.17 to 21.6.17		In Training	
	22.6.17	6am	Company moved to Billets at ST MOMELIN.	A
	23.6.17 to 30.6.17		In Training	

M.H.Senior Major
Comdg. 152nd M.G. Coy.

Army Form C. 2118.

WAR DIARY

INTELLIGENCE SUMMARY

152nd Machine Gun Coy.

Vol 19

(Erase heading not required.)

Instructions regarding War Diaries and Intelligence Summaries are contained in F.S. Regs., Part II. and the Staff Manual respectively. Title Pages will be prepared in manuscript.

Place	Date	Hour	Summary of Events and Information	Remarks and references to Appendices
	1.7.17		Coy. in training at ST MOMELIN.	
	2.7.17		Transport moved by road to WORMHOUDT.	
	3.7.17		Coy. moved by tactical train from ST OMER to POPERINGHE and marched to "D" Camp, A 30 Central	
	5.7.17		"B", "C" and "D" Sections – 12 Guns – relieved 155? M.G. Coy. in line at ST JULIEN. "A" Section – 4 guns at Transport Lines.	
	8.7.17		"A" Section relieved "C" Section which proceeded to Transport Lines	
	9.7.17		"B" " "D" " " " " " CANAL BANK.	
	10.7.17		Casualties in line – 12 O.R.	
	11.7.17		Transport moved by road from POPERINGHE to ZERMEZEELE.	
	12.7.17		" " " " ZERMEZEELE to KINDERBELCK.	
	13.7.17 to 22.7.17		Coy. relieved by 164th M.G. Coy – 12 Guns – and moved to "D" Camp, "A" Central. Coy. moved by bus from A.30. Central to KINDERBELCK Coy. at KINDERBELCK training on model scheme for future operations	
	23.7.17		Transport moved by road to WORMHOUDT.	
	24.7.17		" " " " from WORMHOUDT to A. 30 Central.	
	28.7.17 to		Coy. moved by bus from KINDERBELCK to "D" Camp, A 30 Central.	
	30.7.17		Preparing for offensive operations. 16 guns moved into positions for assembly in line at ST JULIEN.	
	31.7.17		Attack. A full account will be given next month.	

Capt.
Commdg. 152nd Machine Gun Company.

SECRET

War Diary.

1st August 1917.
TO
31st August 1917.

152nd Machine Gun Company.

Army Form C. 2118.

WAR DIARY

INTELLIGENCE SUMMARY

(Erase heading not required.)

Instructions regarding War Diaries and Intelligence Summaries are contained in F. S. Regs., Part II. and the Staff Manual respectively. Title Pages will be prepared in manuscript.

Place	Date	Hour	Summary of Events and Information	Remarks and references to Appendices
In the Field	31.7.17		Action of this Company in ST. JULIEN attack in attached herto.	
	1.8.17		Coy. retired in line by 154th M.G. Coy. and returned to A.30 Central.	R.I.P.
	4.8.17		" moved to SIEGE Camp, transferred clothing at HOSPITAL FARM	
	8.8.17		" " ST JANSTER-BIEZEN (SCHOOL CAMP) by road	
	9.8.17 to 28.8.17		Coy in training at ST JANSTER-BIEZEN.	R.I.P.
	29.8.17		Coy moved to REIGERSBURG by train from POPERINGHE and then marched to MURAT FARM. Transport moved to B.28.b.4.3. (CHATEAU des TROIS TOURS) Coy. relieved 32 Coy in line at CANAL BANK and found parties. 8 guns were in reserve at CANAL BANK	R.I.P.
	31.8.17		Coy still in line. Casualties Nil.	

John Fife Lewis
for Capt.
Comdg. 152nd Company M.G.C.

I. The Company assembled in position on the evening of the 30th July at Point "A". All 16 Guns were to go into action, 8 for Barrage Work, 8 for Consolidation.

ASSEMBLY ETC

48 Attached men were lent by the Brigade for carrying purposes — 32 for the Barrage Guns & 16 for the Consolidation Guns. 14 Belt Boxes per Gun were carried by the Barrage Guns & 8 Belt Boxes by the Consolidation Guns. A good supply of Water & Oil was carried.

II. COMMUNICATIONS

The Brigade was laying down in the earlier part of Operations a good line to Point "H." & it was then decided to keep Signallers at this point & rely on Runners to take Messages to the Guns.

III. MOVEMENT OF BARRAGE GUNS

Zero was at 3.50 a.m. On word being received that the Blue Line was captured, the Barrage Guns were sent forward at 6 a.m. to point "B" & they sent forward Scouts to BLACK LINE & received report that this Line was captured by us. They proceeded to point "C". During this latter stage of the journey they passed through an enemy barrage & sustained about 15% casualties. 2 Guns receiving direct hits. Arriving at point "C" the teams dug in, the exact position being made with a view to direct fire, the right flank especially being watched as KITCHENER'S WOOD, which was considered to be a strong obstacle, lay

2.

lay just over a rise on the right. It is to be noted in passing that the old enemy line through HORST PARK & the buildings in the neighbourhood were being constantly shelled by the enemy, (illustrating the value of keeping off the map.)

Lieut. G. S. RIGG D.S.O. who was in command of the Barrage Battery was killed at 8 p.m.   2nd. Lieut W. A. GRASBY was wounded in the earlier stages of the operations but remained at duty.

IV.
MOVEMENT OF CONSOLIDATION GUNS

At 6.30 a.m. 2 Consolidation Guns were sent forward to "D1" under a Sergeant. On reaching positions the Sergeant found that this ridge of ground running through KLEIST & KITCHENER'S WOODS restricted his field of fire & he proceeded forward to "D2".

No casualties were sustained by these 2 teams.   At 10 a.m. the situation having cleared itself somewhat on the GREEN LINE the remaining 6 guns were sent forward & took up positions in pairs at "E","F" & "G1".

At 10.15 a.m. the Standing Barrage had ceased. In spite of this however, and a good deal of sniping from Machine Guns & Rifles the 6 guns got into position without casualties.

V.
ACTION OF BATTERY

A good supply of S.A.A. Boxes was brought up to point "H" by mid-day & the Battery therefore was well supplied in all respects.   No S.O.S. calls were received until 5.30 p.m. & the call then was somewhat on the left flank.   In the meantime it had been officially reported to the O.C. Battery that we had no troops over the STEENBECK. & the

3.

the barrage line was brought down from "K1" (original line) to "K2". Nothing developed on the Divisional Front. Another S.O.S. call was put up at 9.15 p.m. when the guns once more opened out on "K2". No organised attack however seemed to develop on this Division's Front. To prevent enemy from digging any further lines or making sniping posts in the fairly numerous trees, harassing fire was kept up during the night. The number of rounds fired was 20,000. With regard to Consolidation guns at "G1", these obtained a good many targets on small parties of the enemy on the left flank. Range between 800 & 1000 yards. 1,000 rounds were fired by these two guns & they had subsequently to alter their position to "G2" as the enemy had observed their position due to the firing.

VI.   The weather broke down during the night of 31st July/1st August & continued to rain heavily through the day of 1st August.   Nothing new

RELIEF   developed & the Coy. was relieved about 6 p.m. The Divisional Company taking over the Barrage Battery & 8 guns of the 154th Coy. relieved the Consolidation Guns.   Tripods, belts & belt boxes, S.O.S. lights, water & extra rations being handed over to the incoming teams

4.

teams. Detailed casualties of the Coy. were -

   1 Officer Killed
   3 Other Ranks Killed
   9 Other Ranks Wounded
  & 4 Other Ranks Missing.

       [signature] Capt.

H PILCKEM 1/10,000

WAR DIARY

INTELLIGENCE SUMMARY

152 M.G. Coy
Vol 21

Army Form C. 2118.

(Erase heading not required.)

Place	Date	Hour	Summary of Events and Information	Remarks and references to Appendices
In the Field	1.9.17		Company in Line in front of POELCAPPELLE.	N.P.
	6.9.17		Company relieved by 154th Coy. M.G.C. Casualties in Line 1 O.R. Company moved to "D" Camp A.30 Central.	N.P.
	11.9.17		Company less 2 O/R's and Orderly Room moved to MENTQUES for Field Firing practice at GUÉMY.	N.P.
	14.9.17		Company returned to "D" Camp from MENTQUES.	N.P.
	18/19.9.17		8 guns under 1 Officer and 12 O.R's moved to FERDINAND FARM to take up Barrage positions.	Appendix "A"
	19.9.17		Remainder of gun personnel moved up to positions	N.P.
	20.9.17		Attack on PHEASANT FARM, PHEASANT TRENCH and BLOCKHOUSES Casualties 1 O.R.	N.P.
	23.9.17		Company relieved 154th Coy. in line. 16 guns used.	N.P.
	24.9.17		Company relieved by 32nd Coy. M.G.C. Casualties OR. 1 K. 1 D of W. 8 W. Company moved to SIEGE CAMP.	Appendix "B"
	29.9.17		Company moved by tactical train from ROODPOUTRE to BAUPAUME	N.P.
	30.9.17		Arrived at BAPAUME and marched to ACHIET-le-PETIT area.	N.P.

1/10.17 Comdg 152) Company. M.G.C.

R.H. Pyle. Lieut

Appendix II

Report on Action of Barrage Batteries during recent Operations.

1. Eight Guns of the 152nd Machine Gun Coy. were utilised to fire a harassing barrage on the morning of 20/9/17.

2. The Guns were grouped into two batteries of 4 guns each & named P1 & P2.
P1 Battery was located at C.5.c.1.7.
P2 " " " " C.4.b.5.2

3. The Guns were brought up to positions stated on night 18/19th/9/17 under One Officer, two effective tanks per four guns and one man per team. The guns were laid on Barrage Lines at dawn 19/9/17 as follows:-

	TARGET.	COMPASS BEARING	Q.E.
P1 Battery	V 35.c.0.7. V 25.c.30.35" to V 25.a.30.05. V 25.c. 55.45.	75½°M to 84½°M.	3.48
P2 Battery	U.30.b.35.90 U.30.b.75.20. to U 24.d 55.00 U 30.b.9.3.	70½°M to 79½°M.	4.16

4. Remainder of personnel, bringing total up to 2 Officers, 2 effective tanks per 4 guns & 4 men per team moved up to position on afternoon of Y day.

5. The personnel mentioned in 3 fired practice barrages on these targets from 8.37 am to 8.58 am 19/9/17 when 4750 rounds were fired and from 5.36 pm to 5.58 pm. 19/9/17 when 4,500 rounds were fired.

6. Guns were relaid on barrage lines at 6.50 pm. 19/9/17.

7. Zero hour was at 5.40 am. 20/9/17. P1 & P2 batteries fired from Zero to Zero + 7 mins.
   Ammunition fired 10,000 rounds.

8. Enemy barrage opened at 5.44 am. Light Barrage fell on STEENBECK area.

9. Casualties – 1 man wounded.

10. After firing barrage P1 Battery fell into Bde. reserve and was subsequently utilised for consolidation purposes. P2 battery bivouac at C.4.b.5.2. the guns being mounted for Anti Aircraft duty.

General.

1. Dumps of S.A.A & water had been formed at positions prior to this Coy. occupying them.

2. During night 18/19th/9/17. P1 & P2 batteries were shelled at intervals by 5.9" and heavy shrapnel.

John Pyle Lieut
Comdg. 152nd Machine Gun Coy

Appendix "B" to September War Diary.

16 Guns of the 152nd Machine Gun Coy. relieved 16 Guns of the 154th M.G. Coy. on the night of 21/22 - 9 - 17. 12 Guns were used for consolidation & took up positions with field of fire as shewn on attached tracing to superimpose on Map of POELCAPPELLE 1/10,000 Ed. 3. The remaining 4 Guns were used for Anti-Aircraft their position being at C.4.b.5.2 The Company was relieved on the night of 24/25 - 9 - 17 & returned to SEIGE CAMP The personnel of the 12 consolidation guns received only 1 Casualty (1 O.R. Killed) whilst in their positions & Sustained 1 Died of Wounds 8 wounded in getting in & getting out of positions.

REP:- Poelcappelle 1/10,000
Ed. 3.

Identification Trace for

SECRET

Vol 22

War Diary
for
October 1917.
of
152ⁿᵈ Coy M.G.C.

CONFIDENTIAL
No 21(A)
HIGHLAND
DIVISION.

Army Form C. 2118.

WAR DIARY

INTELLIGENCE SUMMARY

(Erase heading not required.)

Instructions regarding War Diaries and Intelligence Summaries are contained in F.S. Regs., Part II. and the Staff Manual respectively. Title pages will be prepared in manuscript.

Place	Date	Hour	Summary of Events and Information	Remarks and references to Appendices
In the Field	1st		Coy. in training at Achiet-le-Petit.	
	6th		Coy. and Transport moved to M.16.b. (CARLISLE LINES) by march route.	
	6th to 12th		Q.M. Stores at M.29.a. (SWINDON STATION).	
	13th		Coy. in training.	
	15th		Coy. moved to NORTHUMBERLAND LINES.	
	16th		14 guns moved up to line (CHERISY) under a guard. Personnel of Coy. relieved 153rd Coy. in line.	
	to 31st		18 Guns on Bde. front, 16 of 152nd Coy. and 2 of 232nd Coy. The Guns were distributed in depth, 14 in Support and Reserve System, 2 at disposal of Support Bn. Comdr. and 2 at disposal of Reserve Bn. Comdr. Four guns fired nightly an average of 6,000 rounds on enemy communications. One gun mounted in Support for Anti-Aircraft. 4 guns co-operated with Artillery	
	18/19th		ditto.	
	23rd		ditto.	
	26th		ditto.	
	29th		8 guns co-operated in raid by Division on right.	
	30/31st		4 guns co-operated with Artillery	
	31st		Coy. relieved in line by 103rd Coy. and moved to DAINVILLE by bus. (Casualties Nil - for the month)	

Comdg. 152nd Coy. M.G.C.

152nd Brigade.

51st Division.

-------3/4---------

152nd MACHINE GUN COMPANY

NOVEMBER 1917.

Appendix :-

Report on Operations 20th - 23rd.

WAR DIARY
or
INTELLIGENCE SUMMARY.
(Erase heading not required.)

Army Form C. 2118.

Place	Date 1917	Hour	Summary of Events and Information	Remarks and references to Appendices
In the Field	Nov. 1-16.		Company in training at DAINVILLE.	
			Lieut D.G. POTTER joined Coy. from M.G.C. Base Depot.	
	17.		Coy. entrained at BEAUMETZ LES LOGES, detrained BAPAUME, & marched to ROCQUIGNY.	
	18.		Coy. marched to METZ.	
	20.		Coy. assembled in LINE (12 guns) at TRESCAULT for Attack Appendix "A".	
	24.		Coy. Relieved in LINE by GUARDS M.G. Coy. & proceeded to RIBECOURT.	
			Coy. marched to YTRES, entrained for AVELUY & marched to PONTOON PARK near BOUZINCOURT.	
	30.		Coy. marched to ALBERT & entrained for BAPAUME, Marched to BARASTRE.	
			Average Strength of Coy. during Nov. Officers. 10. Other Ranks. 177.	
			Casualties for Nov. R. ------ 5 Other Ranks Wounded.	

Shaw Capt.
Comdg. 153 Coy M.G.C.

Appendix "A"

Headquarters,
152nd. Infantry Brigade.   2151
                                                   26-11-17

Ref. Your G.699/1 of 25/11/17 undermentioned is my report on the Operations 20th Novr. to 26th Novr. 1917.

Para I

20th Novr 1917. The Company went into action with 12 Guns, manned by 7 men & a L/Cpl. each. 4 Guns being man handled & remaining 8 being on Pack ponies.

The reduction in the number of Guns enabled a sufficient supply of S.A.A., water & tools to be taken forward. Practically all guns had 10 boxes S.A.A. in action on 23rd.

Map I showing scheme of consolidation is attached.

Zero Hour was at 6.20 a.m.

At 8.50 a.m., every thing going well, Tanks seen at RAVINE 4 guns carried by men were sent forward.

At 9.30 a.m. Tanks across the Railway Line 8 guns on Pack Animals were sent forward.

At 10.45 a.m. Officer & reconnoitring party discovered FLESQUIERES holding out. Animals had mean time gone towards RIBECOURT & were stopped at Ravine. ARGYLLS reported troops held up & expecting Counter Attack asked for Machine Gun Support. 4 Guns were placed on Railway Line guarding Flank & front of Brigade.

The 4 Guns on foot were got forward to K.24.c.8.2 & L.19.d.1.8.

3.

As afternoon passed & no further progress was made by Infantry, guns were prepared for defence in depth & for overhead fire at night to prevent withdrawal of Field Guns which had held up Tanks. 2 German Guns & S.A.A. were borrowed from the GORDONS to strengthen the Line.

Telephone connection in the meantime had been established with the Brigade & the dispositions were approved. Authority for the harassing fire was obtained at 6.15 p.m. and six guns from then on kept up fire continuously during the dark.

19,000 rounds were fired & it is hoped had some connection with the capture of guns the following morning.

Majority of S.A.A. was obtained from Dump in RIBECOURT. The refilling of belts, carrying of S.A.A. & continuous fire by these guns meant that teams worked practically continuously throughout the night. Rations were brought up at 7 p.m. by Pack Animals & a Field Kitchen which had been captured by the 5th Seaforths & left, after taking the animals out, was taken back. This Kitchen was kept by the Coy. through the courtesy of the 5th Seaforths, and proved invaluable later on in providing soup etc. to the Company.

Casualties 1 man wounded.

2.

22nd Nov 1917.   Orders were issued to go forward with Infantry & consolidate the dotted Red line in accordance with the original scheme.

No opposition being encountered from the enemy, this was done without any hitch. The two forward guns on the right were somewhat heavily shelled on reaching position with light field guns.

An advanced Report Centre was established on the FRESNIÈRES - CROISILLES Road at L.8.c.10.25.   Runners were kept there for each pair of guns & also Runners for Rear H.Q. in FRESNIÈRES.   This arrangement worked well for messages & Rations. Subsequently, surplus men in teams were withdrawn to dug-outs to rest & get hot food.

23rd Nov 1917.   After midnight on night of 22/23rd Orders were received to assemble teams, guns & pack animals in SUNKEN ROAD L1/L9.
4 Guns of 33rd M.G. Coy. were placed under this Brigade and a Scheme of consolidation was arranged in consultation with the D.M.G.O. as per attached Map No.3.

In view of the danger of discovery from aeroplanes authority was obtained at 1.15 a.m. to assemble Pack Animals in BEETROOT FACTORY.

This involved a great deal of re-arrangement during the next 5 hours.   Guns & equipments having to be withdrawn from all parts of the Brigade Front to BEETROOT FACTORY, made ready for putting on Pack Animals and teams taken

forward. Despite a pitch dark night the
operation was carried out correctly & up to time.

The Attack commenced about at 10.30 am.
Tanks were seen entering Fontaine with Infantry
in support and at 11.20 am. orders were given
for 4 guns to go forward, and at 11.35 the
the next 4.

Considering the open nature of the approach
to Fontaine, the weakness of the barrage & the fact
that no attack was being made on the Foret
Wood on the Right it is very doubtful if
Pack Animals should have been used. The
animals were unloaded at the brow of the
hill 26.C. 4 horses were killed & 2 Transport
drivers wounded.

The teams proceeded forward carrying
the Guns: the Right 4 guns & also the 4 guns of
233rd Coy. on finding the Infantry held up,
took up positions in conjunction with the Browning
controlling all the Valleys.

The Left 4 guns followed the Seaforths up
the Edge of the wood under heavy M.G. fire
but had only one Casualty. 38 Belt boxes
were got up here, the men carrying well
despite their exhausted state.

At about 2.30 pm Enemy was seen to be
reinforcing the Village, & all 4 guns opened
fire. Range about 900 yards. Enemy in parties
of about 20: effect could not be seen owing to
the lie of the ground. 500 rounds fired.

About 3.45 pm. the Infantry withdrawing
on the Right Flank, the position here became
somewhat doubtful. However 2 Companies

5.

... of 5th Seaforth, arrived with Tanks and not being able to get forward to FONTAINE, strengthened our position in the S.E. Corner of the wood by digging in alongside the guns.

Advanced Coy. H.Q. were established at F.26.d.7.5.

At dusk, orders were received to open harassing fire on FOLIE WOOD & eastern outskirts of FONTAINE. This was done where possible but the continual movement of our Infantry did not allow of much firing.

The four Reserve Guns had not been moved at this point. On word reaching Brigade of the doubtful position at the S.E. Corner of the wood, 2 of the Guns were sent forward to F.20.c.8.1 and dug in with a Coy. of 7th BLACK WATCH.

The situation had by this time become quiet.

Information was then received that the GUARDS would relieve the whole Sector. The M.G. Coy. arrived without Guns. Authority was received to hand over 8 Guns complete to them, the remaining Guns on the Brigade front to withdraw.

Relief was carried out smoothly, all teams being clear of Sector by dawn.

Total Casualties.

	Horses.		Men.	
	Killed.		Killed	Wounded
152nd Coy. M.G.C.	2.		–	5.
153rd "	–		1	6.

Para 2.

I have no remarks to make under the various headings contained in 7th U.D. Letter No. S.G. 729/504.

28-11-17.

Thom Catt.
Comdg. 152nd Coy. M.G.C.

152nd. Coy. M.G.C.

For the purposes of the War Diary a tracing has been made to superimpose on SHEET 57ᶜ N.E. 1/20,000.

The scheme of Consolidation for the attack on 20-11-17 is shown in RED.

The scheme of Consolidation for the attack on 23-11-17 is shown in BLUE.

The actual positions taken up on 23-11-17 are shown in GREEN.

Capt.,
Comdg. 152nd Coy. M.G.C.

To Superimpose on Sheet. 57C N.E.
1/20,000.

Alternative position
for Reserve Guns

2 guns in
Reserve not
moved

SECRET.

152ⁿᵈ Coy. M.G.C.

WAR DIARY.

FOR

DECEMBER. 1917.

Army Form C. 2118.

WAR DIARY
or
INTELLIGENCE SUMMARY
(Erase heading not required.)

Place	Date	Hour	Summary of Events and Information	Remarks and references to Appendices
In the field. France	1.		Coy. at BARASTRE.	
	3.		Coy. moved to BEUGNY.	
	4.		Coy. moved into Line MEUVRES Sector.	
			12 Guns were placed in the Old British Front Line on the Front of both 153rd & 154th Brigades 3500 yds (4 in Support, and 8 guns (4 from Divisional Cy. & 4 from Resting Brigade) manning positions in the Reserve Line. Three Guns were under command of this Brigade and were given Temporary S.O.S. Lines. The two Brigades retired during the night from positions in HINDENBURG LINE, through this Brigade, without incident. There were no prepared positions for Vickers Guns in the Front Line which was narrow and shallow though well manned. During the next few days several enemy patrols were seen and fired at — but only in one case (1 man wounded) could the effect be observed.	
	5.		Casualties 1 O.R. wounded.	
	8.		A rearrangement was made in the distribution of Vickers Guns as follows:— 7 in front line, 5 in Support, 9 in Support Line and 3 in Corps Reserve Line. Those marked * being supplied by Brigade Cy. in Line.	

WAR DIARY
or
INTELLIGENCE SUMMARY

(Erase heading not required.)

Army Form C. 2118.

Place	Date 1917	Hour	Summary of Events and Information.	Remarks and references to Appendices
In the Field	Nov. 10.		Coy. relieved in line by 153rd Coy, & proceeded to LOCH CAMP, FREMICOURT. (1 gun "D" Section remained in line).	
	12.		"D" Section moved into Reserve Line & relieved 1 gun "H" Section.	
	16.		"A" Section relieved "D" Section in Reserve Line.	
	22.		Brigade moved into the line taking over 2/3rds. only of Divisional Front. Disposition of this Brigades guns was as follows:— 4 in Front Line, 3 in Support, 4 in Reserve Line and 5 at Transport Lines BEUGNY on 1 hours notice.	
	26.		An extra 750 yds. of front to the right was taken over by Brigade. 4 guns of the Divisional Coy. relieved 4 guns of Right Division in 8 Battery Position, conforming with the S.O.S. defences for that Sector. The position also allowed direct fire to be brought on the new front if necessary. Inter-Section relief. Casualties - 1 O.R. Wounded.	
	27. 29.			
	30.		"B" Section moved to MIDDLESEX CAMP, FREMICOURT. Coy. relieved in line by 154th Coy, & proceeded to MIDDLESEX CAMP, FREMICOURT.	Capt. Comdg. 152nd Coy. M.G.C.

Confidential
War Diary
of
152nd. Co. M.G. Corps.
From 1st to 31st. Jan., 1918.

WAR DIARY
INTELLIGENCE SUMMARY.

(Erase heading not required.)

Army Form C. 2118.

Place	Date 1918	Hour	Summary of Events and Information	Remarks and references to Appendices
In the field	Jany 1.		Bqn. in training at MIDDLESEX CAMP. FREMICOURT.	
	4. } 5. }		Bqn. digging new BEAUMETZ – MORCHIES line.	
	7.		Bqn. moved into line. 11 guns relieved 15th Bn. (7 guns) in front line and (4 in intermediate line.) 5 guns at transport lines. BEUGNY on ½ hours notice.	
	8.		Casualties – 1 O.R. (accidentally wounded.)	
	12.		Inter-section relief. 2 guns moved into line as working party on dugouts.	
	15.		Bqn. relieved in line by 15th Bn. (7 guns) + 2/32nd Bn. (4 guns) and moved to MIDDLESEX CAMP. FREMICOURT.	
	16.		Transport moved from BEUGNY to COURCELLES-LE-COMTE. Bqn. marched from MIDDLESEX CAMP. FREMICOURT to COURCELLES-LE-COMTE.	
	17. to 20.		Bqn. under orders of 6th Division. 4 guns ordered to be mounted for protection of village against E.A.	
	21.		Guns, clothing and equipment cleaned and dried – Deficiencies replaced. Commenced 3 weeks Special Training Programme. – Backwise Squad formed + a good deal of Close Order Drill done.	
	28.		Captain CROCKETT. T. to ENGLAND on 9th Instructional Staff Course.	
	29.		Inspection of Bqn. (including transport) by Brigade Commander.	

Comdg 152nd Coy M.G.C.

(6339) Wt. W160/M3016 1,500,000 10/17 McA & W Ltd (E 1898) Forms W3091. Army Form W.3091.

Cover for Documents.

Nature of Enclosures.

War Diaries.

152 Co. M.G.C.
~~1/5th Seaforth Highrs.~~
~~1/6th Seaforth Highrs.~~
~~1/6th Gordon Highrs.~~

From 1st to 28th Feb., 1918.

Notes, or Letters written.

WAR DIARY
or
INTELLIGENCE SUMMARY.
(Erase heading not required.)

Army Form C. 2118

152nd Coy. Machine Gun Corps

Place	Date 1918	Hour	Summary of Events and Information	Remarks and references to Appendices
In the Field	Feb 7.		Coy in training at COURCELLES LE COMTE.	
	8.		Coy (including Transport) inspected by G.O.C.	A/P
	9.		Sub-sections inspected by G.O.C. – Coming into Action from Pack Animals.	A/P
	10.		Coy marched from COURCELLES LE COMTE to FREMICOURT. LIMBER CAMP. Transport at LOCH CAMP, FREMICOURT.	A/P
	11.		Coy moved into Line (16 guns) & relieved 71st M.G. Coy. 8 Guns in Support Line, 8 Guns in Reserve Line.	A/P
	12.		Transport moved to ARTILLERY CAMP.	
	13.		One gun moved from RESERVE LINE to SUPPORT LINE.	A/P
	20.		14 Guns relieved in Line – 13 by 154th M.G. Coy, 1 by 222nd M.G. Coy. 2 guns remained in RESERVE LINE. One relief detachments remained at ARTILLERY CAMP, FREMICOURT. Anti-aircraft defence of FREMICOURT taken over from 154th Coy M.G.C.	A/P
	21/28		Coy in Divisional Reserve at FREMICOURT.	A/P
	18.		2nd Lieut. J.A.W. MUNTZER joined Coy from M.G.C. Base Depot.	A/P
			Casualties – Nil.	

[signature] Lieut.
Comdg. 152nd Coy. Machine Gun Corps.